YOU CAN DO IT!
★ WORKBOOK ★

DREAM IT ★ WRITE IT ★ DO IT

CHRONICLE BOOKS
SAN FRANCISCO

YOU CAN DO IT! WORKBOOK was inspired by the life and work of
Lauren Catuzzi Grandcolas and created by her friends and family.
Text by Yvette Bozzini and illustrations by Julia Breckenreid.

Proceeds from **YOU CAN DO IT! WORKBOOK** will be donated to the
Lauren Catuzzi Grandcolas Foundation, which supports charitable causes
and scholarships for women.

Copyright © 2005 by Herter Studio LLC
Illustrations copyright © 2005 by Julia Breckenreid
All rights reserved. No part of this book may be repro-
duced in any form without written permission from
the publisher.

Page 3: from *Journal of a Solitude* by May Sarton.
Copyright © 1973 by May Sarton. Used by permission
of W.W. Norton & Company. Quotes on pages 9, 19,
31, 43, 55, 67, 79, 91, 103, 115, and 127 are taken
from *You Can Do It!* by Lauren Catuzzi Grandcolas.
Copyright © 2005 by Herter Studio LLC.

ISBN 0-8118-5152-4

Manufactured in China
Typeset in Berkeley Oldstyle and Knockout

Chronicle Books endeavors to use environmentally
responsible suppliers and materials in its gift and
stationery products.

Distributed in Canada by Raincoast Books
9050 Shaughnessy Street
Vancouver, British Columbia V6P 6E5

10 9 8 7 6 5 4 3 2 1

Chronicle Books LLC
85 Second Street
San Francisco, California 94105
www.chroniclebooks.com

produced in association with:
Herter Studio
432 Elizabeth Street
San Francisco, CA 94114
www.herterstudio.com

Caroline Herter / Producer and Creative Director

Vaughn Lohec and Dara Near / Editorial Advisors

Yvette Bozzini / Writer

Julia Breckenreid / Illustrator

Debbie Berne / Project Manager and Designer

Adrianne Koteen / Editorial Assistant

Kathleen Erickson / Proofreader

So perhaps we write

   toward what we will become

from where we are.

MAY SARTON ★ ★ ★ ★ ★ ★ ★

★ INTRODUCTION ★

In the last year of her life, Lauren Catuzzi Grandcolas passionately pursued a dream—the creation of a book called YOU CAN DO IT!

She knew that women can do anything and everything. The way she lived her life—smiling at new experiences, laughing while learning, embracing rather than avoiding challenges—proved this. But she also knew how easy it is for women to put aside personal dreams in the midst of jam-packed, pulled-in-a-dozen-different-directions days. And she saw that while it might be "easy" to let the things we want to do languish at the never-reached bottom of daily must-do lists, doing so comes at a price. We may be accomplished, efficient, and surrounded by family, friends, and co-workers who rely on us. But aren't we missing out on something *at least* as important if we don't also dare to dream and pursue our passions? If we did, wouldn't it make us happier people, more fulfilled in our friendships, families, and workplaces, able—by pursuing our dreams—to give more to others and inspire them to do the same. And wouldn't life—for the very short time we are here—just be richer, and more *fun?*

Because Lauren thought the obvious answer to all the questions above was "Yes!," she wanted women everywhere to turn their to-do lists upside down, highlighting, boldfacing, and putting check marks next to all the things we're too busy, too tired, and too afraid to do. She *knew* that with a little guidance, a little support, and a few simple steps, we *could do it*, and she dreamed of helping us know, feel, and experience that life-affirming, life-embracing passion, too.

Lauren's dream came true. Women everywhere have connected with YOU CAN DO IT!'s inspiring message, exuberant approach, and gal-to-gal reminder that no one else can dream our dreams; it's up to us to bring them to life. And while finding the time to pursue our special passions will never be easy, Lauren's tragic death reinforces one of her core beliefs, which is that the time is *now!!!*

YOU CAN DO IT! WORKBOOK is the perfect place to begin. It augments YOU CAN DO IT!'s practical approach to achieving your goals with the conviction that writing is central to both dreaming and doing. These pages offer you a place to imagine your dreams, talk back to your fears, record your progress, and applaud your own accomplishments.

Writing has multifaceted powers. Taking the time to perform the slow-down-and-focus act of putting pen to paper helps us:

CONNECT to what we really want, who we really are, what we really feel.

COMMIT to dreams and schemes that become more clear and more real in print.

CELEBRATE how far we've come and where we want to go next.

Whether it's in the form of a journal, a letter, or a list, writing can prompt light-bulb moments of insight, reveal the missing piece of a puzzle, and act as the secret ingredient that makes a cake rise or fall. As May Sarton wrote in *her* journal, *Journal of a Solitude,* "We write toward what we will become from where we are."

Brain researchers studying how the act of writing boosts achievement hypothesize that writing down our goals may train our brains as exercise does a muscle, and that when we record and visualize achievement, we "rewire" pathways that have dead-ended into unproductive ruts. *However* writing works, the important thing is that it does.

Here you'll find plenty of blank space in which to write whatever you like in whatever manner you choose. On the next few pages, you'll find space to write down your WANT-TO-DO LIST, with a questionnaire designed to tease out those long-forgotten dreams. Sprinkled throughout the pages are more food-for-thought exercises and springboards that may prove helpful for getting started, staying the course, and enjoying the journey. At the bottoms of the pages, you'll find an enticing assortment of ideas for future badges, and at the back of the book, you'll find plenty of space to record contact information for the many new friends you'll make along your way.

Many of the badge experts in YOU CAN DO IT!, including firewalker Heather Ash Asmara, advise readers to take the time to write about their experiences before, during, and after an endeavor. Accomplishments gain significance this way; we thus have proof that we did it, and are then more likely to try it—or another new challenge—again. So record your efforts, write about how alternately hard, terrifying, and exhilarating it is for you to step out of your comfort zone. Vent, rail, weep. Are you a visual person? Doodle your way through your experiences, give yourself gold stars, or paste or tape in ephemera that you collect in your travels. As you can see, the possibilities are truly endless.

Just as Lauren's YOU CAN DO IT! dream could not be fully realized without its readers, you will make this workbook work. Our dream is that YOU CAN DO IT! WORKBOOK will unleash the kind of magic that can only occur when you combine your own unique insights and experiences with the YOU CAN DO IT! spirit—and the power of your pen.

So, as Lauren would say, what are you waiting for?! Turn the page and begin to dream it, write it, and do it—right here, right now.

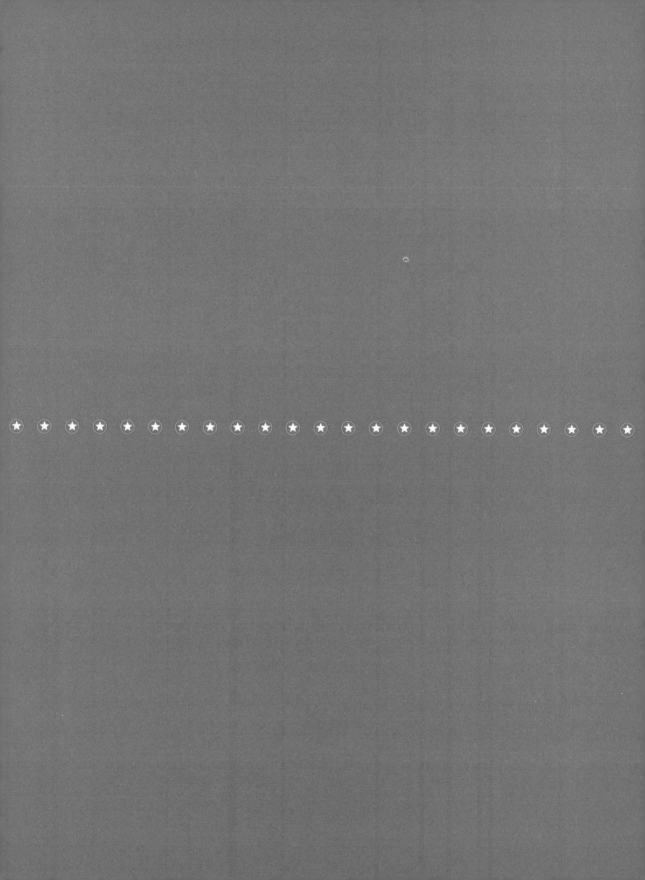

★ ★

START WHERE YOU ARE.

Everything begins

with one step.

NANCY REINISCH, triathlete

★ MY WANT-TO-DO LIST ★

Our lives are such that we can forget about long-neglected dreams or push aside wishes that seem impractical. Whether you're feeling stuck and can't find a place to begin, or you're tingling from a recent accomplishment and hungry for another, try answering these questions designed to help reconnect you with your dreams and passions. Don't think too hard. Try freewriting your responses. This simply means writing without lifting your pen from the paper, the point being to bypass the part of your brain prone to self-censoring and second-guessing—or to forgetting and pushing aside!

What things—that you aren't doing now—did you always think you'd do for sure when you grew up?

_____

_____

_____

_____

_____

_____

_____

Whom do you envy? Why? Write down two or three (or twelve!) things you've envied others for doing.

_____

_____

_____

_____

_____

_____

_____

_____

What do you resolve to do, learn, or try every darn New Year's?

_____

_____

_____

_____

_____

_____

_____

_____

_____

What would you do if you won the lottery, and money and time suddenly weren't an issue?

_____

_____

_____

_____

_____

_____

_____

What would your perfect day entail, from sunup to sundown? Be specific and account for every hour!

_____

_____

_____

_____

_____

_____

_____

_____

Think of your most favorite childhood memories. What did you love doing as a kid?

_____

_____

_____

_____

_____

_____

_____

_____

Now, read your answers. Don't worry if what you've written seems far-fetched or confusing. This is your book. Consider your own words. No matter how fanciful those thoughts, you'll likely find a dream of substance, and from that you can often devise a practical, fulfilling goal. For instance, if you wrote that your favorite childhood memories were running until your sides ached, reading in a secret hiding spot, or fantasizing about far-off lands, you might plan to try a marathon, a book club, or adventure travel.

Don't stop at one round of writing. It's a good idea to go back and do this exercise every now and again. After all, you'll be crossing things off your want-to-do list, and will need to replenish it!

Earn a black belt ★ Herd goats like Heidi ★ Join a hockey team ★ Write a children's book ★

Ride the Trans-Siberian Railway ★ Start a newsletter ★ Throw a vase on a potter's wheel ★

Once you put even a small
change in motion, there's no
telling where the ripple
effect will end.

JULIE SHAH, activist

Be a fiery redhead for a month ★ Start a greeting card company ★ Move to New York City ★

Bake an amazing apple pie ★ Pitch a no-hitter ★ Create a zine ★ Be a foster mom ★

Open a bed & breakfast ★ Win a blue ribbon at the county fair ★ Visit pink dolphins in the Amazon ★

★ SEE YOUR WAY CLEAR ★

Accomplished folk of all kinds point to the power of positive visualization. Athletes will attest that really concentrating on seeing and feeling oneself crossing the finish line or pitching a strike or serving an ace can be just as potent as hours spent physically practicing those moves. Add writing to the mix and you'll boost the power of this prep work.

Try it now. Write down what you'd like to accomplish. Think about each consecutive nut and bolt and write a full paragraph elaborating each step-by-step, chronological detail. Then put down your pen. Sit or lie down, close your eyes, and see yourself doing each step, start to finish. Take your time with this visualization; because many of us find this hard to do, set a timer for five minutes and don't stop until it rings.

Afterward, pick your pen back up and rewrite your initial paragraph, adding in the new details prompted by your visualization. Then, once again, put down your pen, get comfortable, and replay your visualization. Go the full five-minute distance again, and this time, strive even more to feel yourself in action. Now you know the drill; put pen to paper one more time and describe the experience. Chances are you'll have new things to write about.

Also consider: Did you feel tense or fearful during this exercise? See unanticipated rough spots? If so, great! You can plan ahead by taking the time to see and feel yourself gracefully working around these potential pitfalls. And if you simply felt joyous and raring to go during this exercise, go!

Attend local political hearings ★ Go fly-fishing in Montana ★ Adopt a pet from the shelter ★

Host a tea party ★ Bench-press your body weight ★ Visit an active volcano ★ Create your own font ★

★ GO NEGATIVE ★

This may sound counterintuitive, but when you aren't sure what ambition to entertain next, or when your drive is driving you in too many different directions, going negative can be positively galvanizing.

The cranky critic Christopher Hitchens once wrote that while many people remember their first love, he fondly recalls his first hate. Apathy breeds complacency, and since, as a crabby John Lydon (aka Johnny Rotten) once sang, "Anger is an energy," why not pause a moment to reflect on what you *loathe?*

Do you hate not knowing why your computer crashes or cookies crumble? Fume every time you turn on the news or open a 401k statement? Don't just get mad, get moving.

Make a list of things you hate—from war to your wardrobe—and use a red pen for emphasis! Then, with a different colored pen—try purple for power—make like John Lennon and imagine how you'd like it to be different.

An impossible dream? Not necessarily! Now that you're energized, get focused by remembering to make your target goals manageable. As *You Can Do It!* emphasizes, big, pie-in-the-sky ambitions are "baked" one step at a time. So break down and write out the recipe for your purple-pen goal. What ingredients do you need? Supplies? How much time? What are the I, 2, 3, etc., steps? Now here's the procrastination and paralysis-busting key: Only eyeball one step at a time. You can totally do *that!* So jot Step I down in your calendar—in ink (perhaps in a nice, calm shade of blue).

Brew your own beer ★ Volunteer at a homeless shelter ★ Reunite with an old friend ★

Life can grab you when you venture out: One small move can lead to a big break or revelation, and your horizons completely change.

CONNER GORRY, travel writer

Study astronomy ★ Build a robot ★ Start a collection of beach glass ★ Learn to analyze handwriting ★

Weave a blanket ★ Do a ritual fast ★ Clean out your basement ★ Learn Capoeira ★

★ I'M TOO BUSY, TOO OLD, TOO SCARED ★

First, take your pen and cross out the words above. We're not kidding! Words are powerful, and mantras made up of excuses, insecurities, and fears don't help. But we're not naive enough to think that crossing out the words banishes the belief. To do that, it's important to get clear about what you're telling yourself and why.

When we attempt to make a change or try something new, it's easy to get stuck in the mire of anticipation. We spend so much time imagining the worst that could happen, we give up before we get started. The key to turning this worst-case scenario around is listening to your fears and apprehensions, rather than trying to ignore them. That background mind music might be so habitual that you no longer hear it, but that doesn't mean it isn't working to sabotage you. So turn up the volume and remember, the accomplished aren't fearless, they've just learned to feel their fears—and do it anyway.

Try giving your inner pessimist free rein on a page or two. When you find yourself shying away from something, write down the reasons why. Dump all your stinkin' thinkin' down on paper as you formulate, work toward, and face challenges with your goals. Try to unpack, or understand, the fear as much as you can. Is it based on past experience, something that happened years ago, or on the opinions of others? Are those things really appropriate here and now? Rise to your own defense and talk back to those confidence-zappers. Think you're too old? Make a list of people older than you who have accomplished the goal. Too busy or tired? Write down all the pleasurable things you do regularly—taping your favorite TV series and watching it (even if it's in the middle of the night), reading your favorite magazine, baking cakes for your friends' birthdays—and acknowledge the maneuvers you make to find the time. Recognize that against the odds, you can and do find the time and energy to do the things you really want. Feeling too afraid? Face the energy behind your fear and allow it to motivate rather than paralyze you. The adrenaline rush of anxiety is not much different than that of excitement. Let that rush of feeling push you into making one initial phone call, let it scare you into that first tiny baby step, and suddenly, you're on your way!

If, when you tune into it, you find that your internal monologue tends toward "Oh, no" or "What was I thinking?", some reprogramming is in order. There's no point affirming that you're a *Sports Illustrated* swimsuit-issue model or can bench press 180 pounds if you aren't and can't. But get real and, as the song says, "accentuate the positive." Try telling yourself things like "I've done my homework," "I can do my best," or "Gosh, aren't I brave." When these kinds of messages become habitual, you have a built-in support system (you!) and start from a position of strength. So write down your personal hit parade of self-esteem low blows and then write a realistic, true, and optimistic antidote next to each one.

Write a letter to the editor ★ Study kung fu ★ Blow glass ★ Visit every U.S. state ★

Learn to waltz with style ★ Take a class in Indian cooking ★ Visit the Great Wall of China ★

Buy a round-the-world plane ticket ★ Learn to play Texas Hold'em ★ Buy a beach house ★

> Your writing is YOURS—
> your ideas, your effort. That's
> what makes the process
> and the completion
> so satisfying.
>
> LAURIE HENRY, writer

Learn how to paint porcelain ★ Take piano lessons ★ Go mushroom hunting ★

Raise a guide dog for the blind ★ Organize a protest march for something you believe in ★

Cook in a soup kitchen ★ Become a birdwatcher ★ Grow a kitchen herb garden ★

Record an elder's oral history ★ Take a cruise ★ Visit Antarctica ★ See Angkor Wat ★

★ CELEBRATE GOOD TIMES ★

In *You Can Do It!*, every badge activity comes complete with a badge sticker—a tangible reward for a hard-won accomplishment. The reason is simple: It's important to celebrate success. When a baby takes her first step, her parents applaud. As we get older, public appreciation for a job well done is a rarity, and so it falls upon us to create our own ways to celebrate success (after every baby step, if you like!). Tangible rewards make goals worth achieving, so give some thought to how you'd like to celebrate your accomplishments. Treat yourself to a fancy dinner out in that skirt you sewed, take a picture of those pretty flowers that grew from the seeds you planted, or plan a trip to the place where the language you are learning is the native tongue. Mark the date of a significant accomplishment on *next* year's calendar so that it becomes an ongoing celebration/holiday. You get the idea! The point is to spend time showing off a little. Don't just give yourself a mental pat on the back—celebrate! Create a cheering section who are keen to high-five your every move. Let supportive friends, family, coworkers, and teachers know that you need strokes. When you reach a goal or pass a plateau, let them know so that they can say "way to go!"

Next time you finish a badge, toot your own horn by writing yourself a press release or news story touting your experience. Describe yourself in the third person and use lots of adjectives. "On June 23, a sweaty but smiling Jane Doe put her foot in a stirrup, sat tall in her saddle, and guided a gorgeous Appaloosa named Amber round the ring of the Sunshine Stables. The culmination of six weeks of challenging riding lessons, Jane's ride featured ten flawlessly executed minutes spent alternating between a stately walk and a thrilling gallop." The local paper may not find it fit to print, but go ahead and send your "Look what I did!" notice to friends and family.

The important thing is to claim your bragging rights and celebrate your good times so that, like Pavlov's dog, you learn that when you achieve, a treat will follow!

Be real, be sincere, and
people will help you. Your
seriousness and commitment
are contagious.

JONA FRANK, filmmaker

Re-upholster your grandma's sofa ★ Learn to sail ★ Watch the salmon run ★ Study massage ★

Join a co-ed soccer team ★ Put in a home network ★ Study abroad ★ Adopt an adult cat ★

★ PLAN B ★

You're driving along—radio on, windows down, smile on your face. Then a big fat detour sign appears. Disaster? Nope. While some turns of event are unforeseeable, some roadblocks are inevitable, and being prepared for slipups and setbacks can turn stop signs into merely temporary delays.

Anticipating obstacles (from bad moods and failures of nerve to illness, mechanical difficulties, and weather problems) will build your resiliency. You can plan how you'll work around an obstacle, rather than letting it freeze you into a pillar of salt. A Plan B doesn't anticipate or invite failure; it gives you flexible, alternative routes to success.

Write about the internal and external obstacles that have thrown you for a loop in the past. Are you prone to tossing aside your regularly scheduled activities for any and every friend in need? (Or are you a primary caregiver who must, to some extent, go with a flow that you can't control?) Have rain, sleet, or snow derailed your last three exercise routines? Does your computer seem to know when you need it most and pick that moment to act up? Plan for your personal potholes by, for instance, writing and rehearsing your "just say no" script, finding and obtaining the schedules for indoor fitness facilities, or (finally!) creating in-a-pinch backups for your computer system. And if you know that the chances are good that child or elder care will slow you down at least once en route to your goal, build some flexibility into your target dates at the outset. (Giving yourself this permission now can keep you from giving up on the goal altogether later.)

By having a Plan B, you'll have, well, a plan. Detours will be less apt to derail you, and you won't have to waste time or energy berating yourself or cursing fate. You'll simply pick yourself up, dust yourself off, and consult the "what if" section of your dream owner's manual.

What's your Plan B?

Make a soufflé ★ Learn how to pickle ★ Embroider a tablecloth ★ Drive on the autobahn ★

Get away for the weekend by yourself ★ Crochet an afghan ★ Live in a foreign city ★

Volunteer for a local arts board ★ Bike to work for a month ★ Go white-water rafting ★

Make a stained glass window ★ Create a show for Community Access TV ★ Start a cooking club ★

★ CHILL OUT ★

You can't *do* all the time, and taking time to just *be* is actually integral to the process of accomplishment. Rest acts to replenish and restore your reserves of energy and enthusiasm when you're on the go toward a goal. (Think of the way athletes build downtime into their training.)

Ideally, whatever you do to take a break should give your mind a rest. Don't get us wrong. We love the way our brains can think, plan, and analyze. But sometimes our minds can race and whirl to no good end—like a hamster in a cage on one of those exercise wheels!

So get off the wheel every once in a while. Pause. Breathe deeply. Observe your inner and outer status quo. Even if you don't love what you see and feel, calmly acknowledging it prepares you to move beyond it. From this place of acceptance, write about where you're at right now, simply, gently, and calmly. Strive not to editorialize or critique. Just be with it, whatever it is.

Downtime can also consist of change-of-pace activities, so make a list of relaxing things you know work for you: walking, knitting, cleaning out a drawer, making soup—you name it. Don't hesitate to take time for these. Many writers, for example, have come to accept that a few hours spent organizing the spice rack or sorting the recycling isn't stalling; it's *part* of their writing process, a time when ideas incubate, previous efforts solidify, and future achievements take shape.

So give it a rest now and again. Relax. And then return to your go-for-the-goal activities with renewed and refreshed vigor.

Throw a surprise party for a friend ★ Make your own candy ★ Go maple sugaring ★ Whittle ★

Make shadow puppets ★ Make all homemade presents for the holidays ★ Practice the yo-yo ★

If you look at a mountain, it seems impossible—
but if you just think about whether you
can lift and lower your foot,
one step at a time,
you can do it.

ARLENE BLUM, mountain climber

Ask for a raise ★ Cut out sugar ★ Read to the blind ★ Make your own soap ★

Apply for a fellowship ★ Audition for a play ★ Plant a vegetable garden ★ Donate blood ★

★ BRANCH OUT ★

You Can Do It! builds our enthusiasm for trying and doing new things. To reinforce your new habit, go someplace that's out of the ordinary for you. If you never go to modern art museums or to movies by yourself, or if you think of nature the way Fran Lebowitz does—as the unfortunate space between the front door of her apartment building and the back door of a cab—check them out!

The point is to get used to the way new people, places, and things can feed your head, fuel your imagination, fire you up—and be just plain fun. It's just the thing when you're bored and looking for a fresh challenge (and when you need to take an invigorating break from the action at hand).

So brainstorm a list of nearby places you've never been to before and things you've never done. Your branch-out list might look something like this:

- Spend a Saturday morning volunteering with that local nonprofit that restores neglected neighborhood creeks and paths.
- Go to the opera.
- Play "tourist in my town."
- Take photos of that cool old building downtown.
- Take a bus ride on that line I've never tried—and sit by the window!

Bring this journal with you when you go and take notes of what you see and how you feel there. Do you want to learn more about architecture, creek restoration, or Giacomo Puccini? Would you like to spearhead a movement to get more environmentally friendly buses? Ready to write an article about a local landmark? Chances are good that by doing or seeing a new thing or two, you'll wind up with a new dream or two to pursue.

Learn to compost ★ Unplug for a weekend ★ Read Colette—in French ★

Call your favorite radio talk show ★ Take a gondola ride in Venice ★ Work on your serve ★

Learn to do a headstand ★ Fight city hall ★ Make homemade preserves ★

Have a fire drill ★ Learn the Greek gods ★ Reread the book you loved most as a teen ★

Host a foreign exchange student ★ Write a fan letter ★ Look for trolls in Iceland ★

Go to the symphony ★ Do a watercolor portrait of your dog or cat ★ Read *War and Peace* ★

★ LET'S MAKE A DEAL ★

Even the most sophisticated you-can't-fool-me among us can be helped along by some simple mind games. A bit of trickery here, a silent bargain or mental handshake there, or even an ironclad contract (no notary required!).

For instance, a physician we know helped herself quit smoking by making a vow: She would send a big donation to a cause she deemed unworthy if she lit up. (To make her vow harder to weasel out of, she told several close friends about her pledge and asked them to hold her to her word.) Two writers broke through their blocks by agreeing to e-mail each other 250 words first thing each morning. Even if they didn't feel like writing, neither wanted to let the other down—and each came to want to impress her friend and fellow writer! A group of friends planned to fly out of town to attend the wedding of a mutual friend. The wedding reception, they learned, would feature big band music. Too shy to do so individually, the friends took evening swing dance classes together in advance of the big event—and paid for a series up front to bolster their commitment.

Consider your personality traits—laziness, responsibility toward others, frugality— and think about how you can use these to keep you going. Make yourself an offer you can't refuse or cut a deal in which penalties apply. If you pay for the class or agree to meet a friend there, are you less likely to plead exhaustion? Do you feed on competition? Camaraderie? Want to be the star of the dance floor or the belle of the ball? Think about it, then write out the kind of contract you know will work for you. Spell out what you will do, what others (if pertinent) will, what you'll get for following through—and what you'll have to endure if you don't! Take it seriously. Sign and date it, and get the signatures of other key parties or that of a witness to your pledge. Make a deal, sign on the dotted line—and be as good as your word!

It's really never too late to
start or start over.

LINDA RUBIO, horseback rider

Strike up a conversation with a stranger at the coffee shop or bookstore ★ Learn to jump horses ★

Write a poem ★ Visit all the churches in your city or town ★ Begin a daily yoga practice ★

★ WE CAN BE HEROES ★

We hope you'll feel like your own hero whenever you set, pursue, and achieve a goal. And we hope you'll seek out heroic role models—like the mentoring experts in *You Can Do It!*—to light your way. These might be anyone from the "badge buddies" you pursue dreams with to the reference librarian who helped you track down that amazing out-of-print how-to or the historical figure you make your mental mentor.

Also try this exercise: List people you looked up to at various points in your life. Describe them and what you admired. Look for common threads—and consider how your "that's so cool" ideas may have changed over the years. When you need motivation, inspiration, or a fresh dream, you'll likely find it here. (While you're at this, why not contact one or two of these people to get an update on their latest accomplishments and to share your own?)

Speaking of sharing, kick your own heroics up a notch by sharing your experience with others. As it says in *You Can Do It!*, "passing it along is one of the great rewards of learning. . . . Maybe you'll become the mentor to a younger woman or do crafts with an older person, run a workshop or run a race for charity."

Brainstorm ways that you can really own your new skills and knowledge, give them away, and maybe even use them to improve another life. Then get ready to turn up on other people's "most admired people" lists! You can do it!

Ice climb through a glacier ★ Listen to the call to prayer in Syria ★ Dance a waltz in a castle ballroom ★

Study astrobiology ★ Enter a bake-off ★ Hit a bull's-eye in darts ★ Go into therapy ★

It's human to want to
know as much as we can
about who we are.

KATHY HINCKLEY, genealogist

★ CONTACTS ★

The bravest and brawniest know when they need reinforcements. No woman is an island. Who are you gonna call? Going it alone is more often a recipe for disaster than an express train to the top of the heap, so assemble a pit crew, enlist a sherpa or two, and plan your lifeline phone call.

This is the place for the phone numbers and e-mail addresses of your resources, supporters, and trusted think-tank members. You may never need to issue an SOS, but just knowing you're prepared to can give you the calmness and confidence to carry on. And when you're blessed with smooth sailing, it's handy to have people to celebrate with at your fingertips!

name ....

address ....

....

phone .... cell ....

e-mail ....

comments ....

....

....

name ....

address ....

....

phone .... cell ....

e-mail ....

comments ....

....

....

name ....

address ....

....

phone .... cell ....

e-mail ....

comments ....

....

....

name ....

address ....

....

phone .... cell ....

e-mail ....

comments ....

....

....

name ....

address ....

....

phone .... cell ....

e-mail ....

comments ....

....

....

name ....

address ....

....

phone .... cell ....

e-mail ....

comments ....

....

....

name ....

address ....

....

phone .... cell ....

e-mail ....

comments ....

....

....

name ....

address ....

....

phone .... cell ....

e-mail ....

comments ....

....

....

name ....

address ....

....

phone .... cell ....

e-mail ....

comments ....

....

....

name ....

address ....

....

phone .... cell ....

e-mail ....

comments ....

....

....

name ....

address ....

....

phone .... cell ....

e-mail ....

comments ....

....

....

name ....

address ....

....

phone .... cell ....

e-mail ....

comments ....

....

....

name ....

address ....

....

phone .... cell ....

e-mail ....

comments ....

....

....

name ....

address ....

....

phone .... cell ....

e-mail ....

comments ....

....

....

name ....

address ....

....

phone .... cell ....

e-mail ....

comments ....

....

....

name ....

address ....

....

phone .... cell ....

e-mail ....

comments ....

....

....

name ....

address ....

....

phone .... cell ....

e-mail ....

comments ....

....

....

name ....

address ....

....

phone .... cell ....

e-mail ....

comments ....

....

....

name ....

address ....

....

phone .... cell ....

e-mail ....

comments ....

....

....

name ....

address ....

....

phone .... cell ....

e-mail ....

comments ....

....

....

name ....

address ....

....

phone .... cell ....

e-mail ....

comments ....

....

....

name ....

address ....

....

phone .... cell ....

e-mail ....

comments ....

....

....

name ....

address ....

....

phone .... cell ....

e-mail ....

comments ....

....

....

name ....

address ....

....

phone .... cell ....

e-mail ....

comments ....

....

....

name ....
address ....
....
phone .... cell ....
e-mail ....
comments ....
....
....

name ....
address ....
....
phone .... cell ....
e-mail ....
comments ....
....
....

name ....
address ....
....
phone .... cell ....
e-mail ....
comments ....
....
....

name ....
address ....
....
phone .... cell ....
e-mail ....
comments ....
....
....

name ....
address ....
....
phone .... cell ....
e-mail ....
comments ....
....
....

name ....
address ....
....
phone .... cell ....
e-mail ....
comments ....
....
....

name ....
address ....
....
phone .... cell ....
e-mail ....
comments ....
....
....

name ....
address ....
....
phone .... cell ....
e-mail ....
comments ....
....
....

name ....
address ....
....
phone .... cell ....
e-mail ....
comments ....
....
....

name ....
address ....
....
phone .... cell ....
e-mail ....
comments ....
....

name ....
address ....
....
phone .... cell ....
e-mail ....
comments ....
....
....

name ....
address ....
....
phone .... cell ....
e-mail ....
comments ....
....
....

name ....
address ....
....
phone .... cell ....
e-mail ....
comments ....
....
....

name ....
address ....
....
phone .... cell ....
e-mail ....
comments ....
....
....

name ....
address ....
....
phone .... cell ....
e-mail ....
comments ....
....
....

name ....
address ....
....
phone .... cell ....
e-mail ....
comments ....
....
....

name ....

address ....

....

phone .... cell ....

e-mail ....

comments ....

....

....

name ....

address ....

....

phone .... cell ....

e-mail ....

comments ....

....

....

name ....

address ....

....

phone .... cell ....

e-mail ....

comments ....

....

....

name ....

address ....

....

phone .... cell ....

e-mail ....

comments ....

....

....

name ....

address ....

....

phone .... cell ....

e-mail ....

comments ....

....

....

name ....

address ....

....

phone .... cell ....

e-mail ....

comments ....

....

....

name ....

address ....

....

phone .... cell ....

e-mail ....

comments ....

....

....

name ....

address ....

....

phone .... cell ....

e-mail ....

comments ....

....

....

name ....
address ....
....
phone .... cell ....
e-mail ....
comments ....
....
....

name ....
address ....
....
phone .... cell ....
e-mail ....
comments ....
....

name ....
address ....
....
phone .... cell ....
e-mail ....
comments ....
....
....

name ....
address ....
....
phone .... cell ....
e-mail ....
comments ....
....
....

name ....
address ....
....
phone .... cell ....
e-mail ....
comments ....
....
....

name ....
address ....
....
phone .... cell ....
e-mail ....
comments ....
....
....

name ....
address ....
....
phone .... cell ....
e-mail ....
comments ....
....
....

name ....
address ....
....
phone .... cell ....
e-mail ....
comments ....
....
....

name ....

address ....

....

phone .... cell ....

e-mail ....

comments ....

....

....

name ....

address ....

....

phone .... cell ....

e-mail ....

comments ....

....

....

name ....

address ....

....

phone .... cell ....

e-mail ....

comments ....

....

....

name ....

address ....

....

phone .... cell ....

e-mail ....

comments ....

....

....

name ....

address ....

....

phone .... cell ....

e-mail ....

comments ....

....

....

name ....

address ....

....

phone .... cell ....

e-mail ....

comments ....

....

....

name ....

address ....

....

phone .... cell ....

e-mail ....

comments ....

....

....

name ....

address ....

....

phone .... cell ....

e-mail ....

comments ....

....

....

name ....
address ....
....
phone .... cell ....
e-mail ....
comments ....
....
....

name ....
address ....
....
phone .... cell ....
e-mail ....
comments ....
....
....

name ....
address ....
....
phone .... cell ....
e-mail ....
comments ....
....
....

name ....
address ....
....
phone .... cell ....
e-mail ....
comments ....
....
....

name ....
address ....
....
phone .... cell ....
e-mail ....
comments ....
....
....

name ....
address ....
....
phone .... cell ....
e-mail ....
comments ....
....
....

name ....
address ....
....
phone .... cell ....
e-mail ....
comments ....
....
....

name ....
address ....
....
phone .... cell ....
e-mail ....
comments ....
....
....

name ....

address ....

....

phone .... cell ....

e-mail ....

comments ....

....

....

name ....

address ....

....

phone .... cell ....

e-mail ....

comments ....

....

....

name ....

address ....

....

phone .... cell ....

e-mail ....

comments ....

....

....

name ....

address ....

....

phone .... cell ....

e-mail ....

comments ....

....

....

name ....

address ....

....

phone .... cell ....

e-mail ....

comments ....

....

....

name ....

address ....

....

phone .... cell ....

e-mail ....

comments ....

....

....

name ....

address ....

....

phone .... cell ....

e-mail ....

comments ....

....

....

name ....

address ....

....

phone .... cell ....

e-mail ....

comments ....

....

....